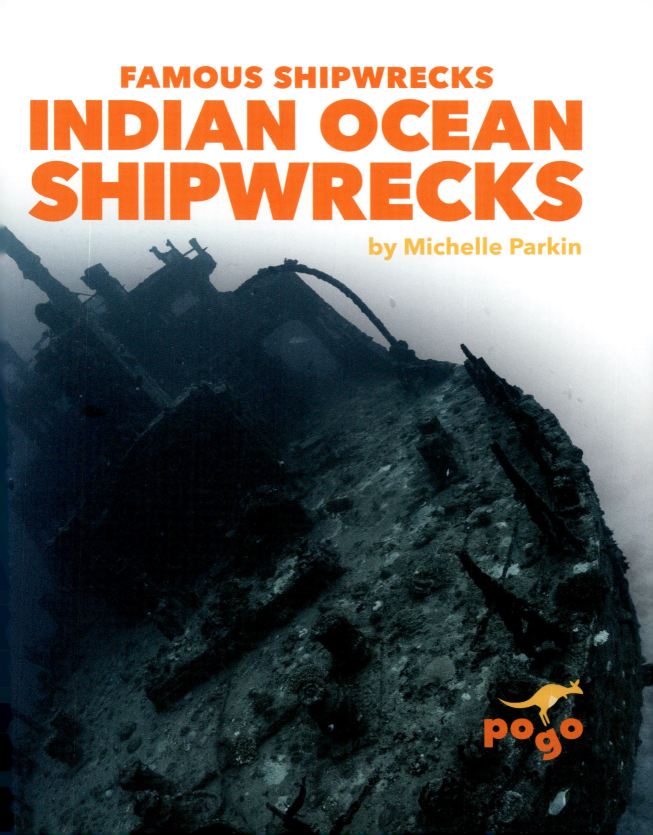

FAMOUS SHIPWRECKS
INDIAN OCEAN SHIPWRECKS

by Michelle Parkin

pogo

Ideas for Parents and Teachers

Pogo Books let children practice reading informational text while introducing them to nonfiction features such as headings, labels, sidebars, maps, and diagrams, as well as a table of contents, glossary, and index.

Carefully leveled text with a strong photo match offers early fluent readers the support they need to succeed.

Before Reading

- "Walk" through the book and point out the various nonfiction features. Ask the student what purpose each feature serves.
- Look at the glossary together. Read and discuss the words.

Read the Book

- Have the child read the book independently.
- Invite him or her to list questions that arise from reading.

After Reading

- Discuss the child's questions. Talk about how he or she might find answers to those questions.
- Prompt the child to think more. Ask: Why are there so many shipwrecks in the Indian Ocean? What can people do to stay safe on the ocean?

Pogo Books are published by Jump!
5357 Penn Avenue South
Minneapolis, MN 55419
www.jumplibrary.com

Copyright © 2024 Jump!
International copyright reserved in all countries. No part of this book may be reproduced in any form without written permission from the publisher.

Library of Congress Cataloging-in-Publication Data is available at www.loc.gov or upon request from the publisher.

ISBN: 979-8-88996-665-4 (hardcover)
ISBN: 979-8-88996-666-1 (paperback)
ISBN: 979-8-88996-667-8 (ebook)

Editor: Alyssa Sorenson
Designer: Anna Peterson

Photo Credits: imageBROKER.com GmbH & Co. KG/Alamy, cover; Huw_Thomas06/Shutterstock, 1; shoricelu/iStock, 3; titoOnz/Shutterstock, 4; Richard Whitcombe/Shutterstock, 5; m.mphoto/Shutterstock, 6; Rasika Muthucumarana - Maritime Archaeology Unit of Sri Lanka, 7; Patrick Baker, WA Museum, TR/A/115, 8–9; Allan C. Green/State Library Victoria, 10–11; Mountains in the Sea Research Team; the IFE Crew; and NOAA/OAR/OER, 12–13; Poelzer Wolfgang/Alamy, 14–15; Reinhard Dirscherl/Alamy, 16–17; STUDIO MELANGE/Shutterstock, 18; Artsiom P/Shutterstock, 19; Nine Below/Shutterstock, 20–21; dushi82/Shutterstock, 23.

Printed in the United States of America at Corporate Graphics in North Mankato, Minnesota.

TABLE OF CONTENTS

CHAPTER 1
Welcome to the Indian Ocean..................4

CHAPTER 2
Swallowed by the Sea...........................6

CHAPTER 3
Sailing the Indian Ocean Today..............18

QUICK FACTS & TOOLS
Where They Sank in the Indian Ocean......22
Glossary...23
Index...24
To Learn More...................................24

CHAPTER 1

WELCOME TO THE INDIAN OCEAN

The Indian Ocean is between Asia, Africa, and Australia. It is the third-largest ocean.

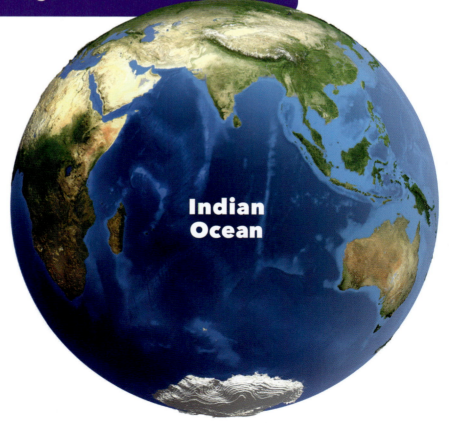

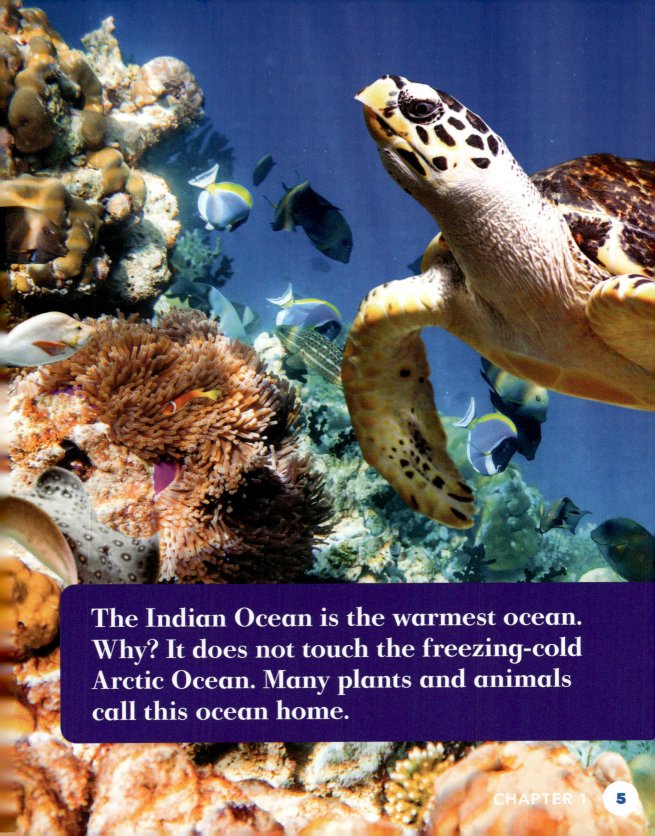

The Indian Ocean is the warmest ocean. Why? It does not touch the freezing-cold Arctic Ocean. Many plants and animals call this ocean home.

CHAPTER 1 | 5

CHAPTER 2

SWALLOWED BY THE SEA

Ships carry goods across the Indian Ocean. But the ocean is dangerous. There are large waves. Violent storms can form in the warm water. Many ships have sunk in the Indian Ocean.

In 2003, a **shipwreck** was found off the coast of Sri Lanka. Divers **explored** it. It was more than 2,000 years old! It is the Indian Ocean's oldest discovered shipwreck.

Sri Lanka shipwreck site

Trial sailed in 1622. The ship was close to western Australia. It crashed into rocks just beneath the water's surface. *Trial* broke apart. More than 100 people died.

Divers found the shipwreck in 1969. How? They saw the ship's anchor. They also saw cannons on the ocean floor.

WHAT DO YOU THINK?

Trial was badly **damaged** after hitting rocks. Why didn't the **crew** see the rocks? What can ships do today to avoid this?

HMAS *Sydney*

CHAPTER 2

HMAS *Sydney* was an Australian warship. It was used during **World War II** (1939–1945). On November 19, 1941, it was sailing close to western Australia. A German ship was nearby. It fired at *Sydney*. *Sydney* fired back. The ships battled at sea!

WHAT DO YOU THINK?

Ships have battled at sea for thousands of years. Why do you think this is?

CHAPTER 2

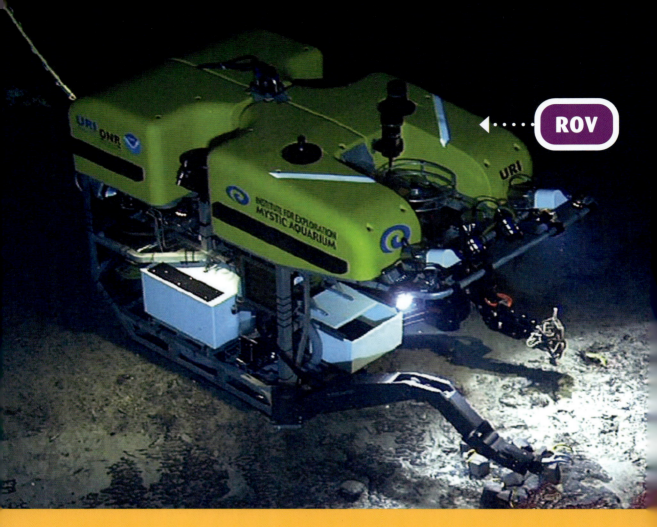

ROV

Both ships were damaged. *Sydney* quickly sank. All 645 people on the ship died. The German ship sank, too. More than 70 Germans died.

Both shipwrecks were found in 2008. People used a **remotely operated vehicle (ROV)** to explore them.

TAKE A LOOK!

ROVs help us explore shipwrecks deep below the ocean's surface. How do they work? Take a look!

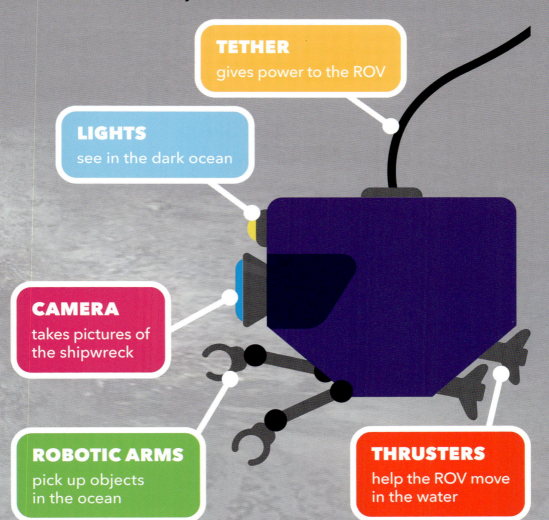

TETHER
gives power to the ROV

LIGHTS
see in the dark ocean

CAMERA
takes pictures of the shipwreck

ROBOTIC ARMS
pick up objects in the ocean

THRUSTERS
help the ROV move in the water

CHAPTER 2

British Loyalty brought oil across the Indian Ocean. In 1942, Great Britain was fighting Japan in World War II. A Japanese **submarine** fired at *British Loyalty*. But the ship did not sink! Two years later, it was attacked again. It still stayed afloat.

In 1946, the British did not want the ship anymore. They sank it. People dive to see the shipwreck today.

DID YOU KNOW?

When the British sank *British Loyalty*, the ship leaked oil. This hurt ocean life nearby.

British Loyalty

CHAPTER 2

In 1981, *Maldive Victory* was full of supplies. It was sailing to the Maldives. This is an island country in the Indian Ocean. The ship smashed into a **coral reef**. Water got into the ship. It sank. Today, divers explore the wreck. Corals cover it.

CHAPTER 3
SAILING THE INDIAN OCEAN TODAY

Today, ships have **radar**. Radar finds nearby ships. **Sonar** helps people find large objects, such as rocks, in the water. These things help ships avoid crashes.

radar

Technology helps people track weather patterns. This helps them avoid sailing through storms, such as **cyclones**. Crews stay in contact with people on land. Using high-tech radios, they call for help if they need it.

cyclone

People search for shipwrecks in the Indian Ocean. They study the wrecks. They learn about the ships and the people who sailed them. Who knows what they will find next?

Stella Maru

CHAPTER 3

QUICK FACTS & TOOLS

WHERE THEY SANK IN THE INDIAN OCEAN

1. A shipwreck was found off the coast of Sri Lanka in 2003. It is more than 2,000 years old.

2. *Trial* sank on May 25, 1622. It crashed into underwater rocks near western Australia. The shipwreck was found in 1969.

3. HMAS *Sydney* battled a German ship at sea in 1941. Both ships sank. The wrecks were found in 2008.

4. *British Loyalty* was damaged many times. It finally sank in 1946. It is now a popular diving spot.

5. On February 13, 1981, *Maldive Victory* hit a coral reef and sank. Divers now explore the site.

GLOSSARY

coral reef: A long line of coral that lies in warm, shallow water.

crew: A group of people who work on a ship.

cyclones: Storms with very strong winds that often have a lot of rain.

damaged: Harmed.

explored: Traveled and discovered things.

radar: A system used to find aircraft, ships, and other objects by reflecting and receiving radio waves.

remotely operated vehicle (ROV): An unmanned underwater machine used to explore deep ocean water.

shipwreck: The remains of a sunken ship.

sonar: A device or method to find out how deep the water is or where underwater objects are.

submarine: A ship that can travel underwater.

World War II: A war in which the United States, Australia, France, Great Britain, the Soviet Union, and other nations defeated Germany, Italy, and Japan.

QUICK FACTS & TOOLS

INDEX

anchor 8
Australia 4, 8, 11
battled 11
British Loyalty 14
cannons 8
coral reef 17
crashed 8, 18
crew 8, 19
cyclones 19
divers 7, 8, 14, 17
explored 7, 12, 13, 17
German 11, 12
Japanese 14
Maldive Victory 17
radar 18
remotely operated vehicle (ROV) 12, 13
rocks 8, 18
sonar 18
Sri Lanka 7
storms 6, 19
submarine 14
Sydney 11, 12
Trial 8
waves 6
World War II 11, 14

TO LEARN MORE

Finding more information is as easy as 1, 2, 3.

1. Go to www.factsurfer.com
2. Enter "IndianOceanshipwrecks" into the search box.
3. Choose your book to see a list of websites.

24 QUICK FACTS & TOOLS